Asatru

A Beginner's Guide to
Modern Heathenism

Table of Contents

Introduction

Heathens, Pagans, and Norse Magic is just for the films and television, right? Well, it may surprise you to know that the old ways and ancient religions are having a resurgence. Modern religious practices are still prevalent, but some people are looking for a more natural way of connecting with their spiritual sides. Should religion be dominated by strict rules and condemnation? Pagans and heathens believe in a kinder way of living. They recognize that powers exist in the universe and beyond that can enhance our lives here in the mortal world.

You may believe that the Gods are out there and you may be interested in finding out more about an alternative way of living. No matter what your reasons, this book will help you understand the basic principles involved in Asatru practices and how they can influence your life. The Asatru people don't believe in preaching;

they simply invite you to become involved. Understand what beliefs they uphold and the rituals they hold to celebrate their Gods. Come on in and consider what a simpler, more heathen existence could hold for you.

Chapter 1:

What is Asatru?

The first centuries of Icelandic history reveal that the primary religion of the area was Asatru. Followers embraced the Paleolithic characteristics, including the Shaman form of the god Odin and the Trickster aspects of his companion Loki. The religion focused on the two main ethics that were common among the warring communities, honor and shame. There was no middle ground for early followers of Asatru; they believed that the only honorable death was on the battlefield.

As settlers chose to traverse Europe before settling in Iceland, it became clear that they brought with them a different type of religion. Early Christian settlers brought a more humane aspect to religious practice, and the nation was divided. In the year 1000 AD, the Viking commonwealth decreed that Iceland was to become a nation that practiced

Christianity but still recognized the ancient religion Asatru.

Two legal codes were put in place to allow the two sets of practitioners to live side by side to avoid a divided nation. Asatru followers, however, felt the need to practice in secret and the religion soon became an underground movement.

In other parts of Europe, the religion continued to flourish until the mid-14th century when Lithuania became the last surviving bastion. There were underground movements like the Odin brotherhood, but on the whole, Europe had chosen to embrace Christianity as the religion of its people.

Odin and Thor still managed to exert influence on other religions. They appeared in texts relating to Shiva and Indra in various forms and continued to be honored by practicing pagans worldwide. In Sweden, a site known as Trolls church was the site for pagan worship for hundreds of years after the nation converted to Christianity, but on the whole, Asatru remained underground.

In the early 20th century, Germanic pagan groups began to emerge and become popular with

German citizens. This led to some early members of the Nazi party pursuing the members of Pagan groups with the intention to persecute them. Although the practice was discouraged by the party, it is believed that many members of such groups were captured and killed in the concentration camps.

In 1973 Iceland underwent a religious revolution, albeit on quite a small scale! A small group of people had been meeting for some time to practice the beliefs and virtues of Asatru and requested recognition by the government. This led to the momentous new holiday entitled "The First Day of Summer," which is celebrated to highlight the end of winter and the beginning of summer in a pagan form.

Although the original group numbered just 12 members, they began to attract attention from other Icelandic people. Their membership grew, and in the early part of 1992, they formed an official branch of their Pagan association. They held their first formal ceremony in June of that year to mark Midsummer Night.

It is currently Iceland's fastest-growing religion with a membership that exceeds 1% of the national population. Now, that may not seem like a huge figure, but the growth of Paganism has risen by over 240% in the past decade, which is pretty spectacular. Asatru is now the 6th largest religion in the region and is also the largest non- Christian doctrine.

Why is Asatru so Popular?

The reasons seem to be multiple. Asatru celebrates ancient rituals and beliefs and invites others to join these celebrations. They hold weekly meetings that are open to the public. Their ceremonies take place at significant times in the Pagan calendar and are called blots. These are also open to the public and are joyful occasions filled with music and traditional dancing. Members are not asked to pray to or be subservient to their Gods, but they are encouraged to ask for their intervention. Gods are more like companions and will never judge their human counterparts.

Asatru doesn't believe in converting people or using missionary tactics to increase its membership. It refuses to lay down dogmas or scriptures to govern how its followers behave. Instead, it encourages members to read and learn from the writings of scholars named the Eddas that were written in the 13th century.

Asatru is a religion that follows the Pagan beliefs that nothing is as important as nature and harmony. It encourages its followers to live a harmonious life, celebrating the wonders of the natural world and embracing ancient beliefs. It refuses to have negative views about other religions and considers itself to be the religion of peace and respect. It does embrace the modern ideals of conservation and environmental nurturing.

While some Pagan groups around the globe claim to be Viking orientated, they choose to glorify the negative aspects of historical events. They promote the violence, militarism, and masculine dominance they interpret as Viking beliefs, and this can lead to incidents of intolerance and racism.

True believers of the Asatru religion shun these Aryan based beliefs and have received hate mail and negative feedback from other groups. In Iceland, the leader of the indigenous branch of Asatru cut all ties to foreign pagan groups who practiced hateful and negative practices back in 1991. True Asatru beliefs are based on love, tolerance, and acceptance. In 2010 the Icelandic government-sanctioned same-sex marriages and couples from across the world traveled there to take part in traditional Asatru marriages.

There are now branches of religion across the world. Anyone can join, and participation is encouraged. In Iceland, anyone can practice the beliefs regardless of race, color, gender, or sexual preference, but if you want to join the official Asartuarfelagio, then you must be a citizen of Iceland or own a home there. Pagans are making a comeback, and Iceland is at the fore of the new movement. They provide a breath of fresh air in a society that seems to thrive on negativity, intolerance, and hate.

Chapter 2:

Norse Gods of Asatru

While some religions prefer their believers to prostrate themselves before their deities, Asatru followers never kneel or bow to their Gods and Goddesses. Instead, they stand tall and hold themselves in a proud and strong stance before them. Rather than worship, they believe that respect and honor should be shown to these ancient ancestors who went before them.

The Gods and Goddesses are considered extended family and are treated as such. They provide guidance and strength and sometimes walk among us in the physical world. They are not considered mystical and unapproachable; they are true and real. They stay close to us so they can provide a worthy council when required.

While there are numerous Gods connected to the Germanic beliefs and the Asatru religion, we will consider the more important ones to begin with. Studying these main deities will help establish the strengths and values they bring to the faith.

Odin: Wednesday is Named After Him (Woden Day)

Possibly the best-known example of ancient Gods, he is the one who takes part in affairs that center around human beings. He is known as the god of magic, wisdom, poetry, and death. His mother and father were both Giants and was named Odin in the old Norse language. He fathered children with his wife Frigga and with Jord, a goddess of the Earth. This union produced Thor, another of the most powerful Gods in Asatru.

Odin has just one eye that produces powerful lights that resemble sunlight. He sacrificed his other eye to take a drink from the Well of Wisdom, which gave him the knowledge to practice the art of necromancy. His residence in Valhalla allows him to observe all the happenings in the 9 worlds that make up the Germanic world.

He is known as the capricious god who can be prone to fury. He tests his followers by creating shamanic reactions and invoking his personal rage to test their self-control and discipline. He will appear to humans as a tall, slender man with a gray beard and a hat that masks his missing eye. He will often be accompanied by 2 wolves named Freki and Geri, and they consume all his food because Odin doesn't eat; he survives solely on wine!

Thor: Thursday is Named After Him, (Thor's Day)

The sky god is often seen wielding a hammer and controls the weather; he has the power to give rain to the farmers to help their crops. He is also called the god of the common man and is considered the guardian of the Earth.

Asatru and other heathen religions depict a powerful god riding through the heavens during a thunderstorm directing the lightning through his hammer. Thunder occurs whenever his hammer is successfully used to target his opponents.

While the hammer of Thor is a powerful weapon, it can also be used for more traditional blessings. It is used to bless the altars in marriage and burial ceremonies, and the Vikings often called on Thor to hallow their precious runes.

His physical incarnation would often be a large blond man with flaming eye sockets and a red beard. However, Thor rarely meddled in human affairs and is more attributed to fighting Giants. He is commonly known as the Thunder God, the Hallower, and the Chariot God, among other names. He is commonly seen as God's protector, and he will work tirelessly to protect them from all forms of harm.

Tyr: Tuesday is Named After Him (Tyr's Day)

The god of battle, sacrifice, and justice. Once known as the most powerful God of Nordic, he was superseded by Odin when he discovered the runes. He is depicted as a one-handed man who proved his bravery by placing his hand in the mouth of the Fenris Wolf. This pledged him to the wolf, and he was the sole god who dared to feed it as it grew. Eventually, the gods turned to the dwarves to fetter the wolf, and the pledge that Tyr had formed with it played an important part in the outcome.

Loki

Loki is the blood brother of Odin, which leads to his inclusion among the ancient gods. In reality, Loki is a Giant lord with the ability to shapeshift and can change his form and sex with ease. He is renowned for his sense of mischief and, in some myths, is helpful if a touch is capricious. He has been described as a trickster god who accompanies Odin wherever he goes. Odin refused to drink wine without Loki being served a cup and, as such, made him a usurper type figure that was rarely offered any form of sacrifice.

Loki also has a dark side and is proclaimed as the God of chaos and change. This defies the values that accompany the Asatru religion, but believers look to Loki to teach them how to change for the better. There is no clear "all good" or "all bad" when considering Loki; he is a fire spirit and as such a complex and anarchic figure. He was bound and tied to three rocks as punishment for plotting against the gods, and his writhing in pain causes earthquakes in the earthly world. Eventually, he will break free and will lead an attack against the

Gods that will result in the final battle that will signal the end of the world. Ragnarök is the name of this battle and a time for reckoning for all the Gods and Goddesses.

These four Gods are just the tip of the iceberg when it comes to studying the deities worshipped by the Asatru. It is important to keep studying them and the tales that accompany them as they are a key part of understanding the beliefs and values they uphold. Other important figures include Baldur, Bragi, and Mimir.

Chapter 3:

Norse Goddesses

In the Asatru religion, the female gods are revered as mothers, wives, and mistresses of the gods. They bear children that are destined for greatness, and they serve alongside their menfolk with power and honor. In this part of the book, we will examine some of the more prominent goddesses that feature in Asatru tales and other Germanic myths.

Frigg or Frigga

Also known as Fricka or Freya, the matron goddess of the home. She is the wife of Odin and mother of three of his sons. Her beloved son Baldur is considered one of the brightest and beautiful of the gods and is the shining embodiment of hope.

Frigg is the goddess of fertility and motherhood, as she represents the strong bonds of marriage and dedication to keeping a home for her husband and children. She is represented by the symbol of the distaff and spindle, which she uses to spin her own materials and create her signature threads.

She is also blessed with the power of foretelling the future, but very rarely shares her knowledge with others. Much about Frigg is steeped in mystery, and she is sometimes depicted as multiple entities that originate from scholastic versions of early Germanic sources.

There is no doubt that Frigg is the highest of all the goddesses, and, as the wife of Odin, this is a place she richly deserves.

Idun

In the ancient Norse language, she was known as Iounn, which translates to "the rejuvenator" and is considered the goddess of youth and immortality. She has the power to grant immortality to humans and to sustain her fellow dwellers in Asgard with the same power. She is endowed with mystical apples that fuel her fellow gods and sustain their powers, making her an important part of the religious conglomerate.

Idun is the keeper of the apples of Idun, which she keeps in a golden casket. She has a physical appearance of great beauty, and her long blonde hair and youthful appearance are well documented. Her marriage to Bragi, the god of poetry and music, was blessed by the gods, and their faces are said to shine with immortal youth, and their eyes are blazing with power. Truly a marriage made in the heavens!

Hel

The queen of the underworld and ruler of the realm of the dead called Helheim. In Viking times, if you died from illness, old age, or other non-battle related way, you were considered a coward and sent to this realm. Only brave heroes and warriors were granted entrance to Valhalla and Asgard.

Odin himself threw Hel down from the sky and cast her into the underworld to rot. She took her place as queen and has ruled there ever since. She is the daughter of Loki and has two siblings, one of whom is the Fenrir Wolf, who took the hand of Tyr. As such, she is not strictly classed as a goddess but deserves mention because of the importance of her role in the underworld.

Her physical appearance is a mix between the living world and the underworld. She appears as a decomposing face that is part flesh and part blue colored. Her body is that of a living woman with the thighs and legs of a corpse. Unsurprisingly, she has a gloomy countenance and a downcast look. Some believers feel that Hel is the most powerful of all the gods because of the decisions she makes, which decide the fate of the human souls who are sent to the underworld.

Freya

The goddess of fate and destiny was born into the Vanir tribe of Norsemen alongside her twin brother Freyr. He was associated with the elves and oversaw the important rites associated with harvest and marriage celebrations. His sister Freya epitomizes pleasure and opulence. Depicted in myths as a blond lady with flowing locks and a youthful face, she can often be seen driving a chariot pulled by cats.

This association is because she could manipulate others and alter their desires and hopes, much like her feline companions! She is associated with an alternative form of the afterlife called Folkvang, which allowed her to choose which warriors slew in battle joined her and which were sent to Valhalla.

Fulla

The goddess of secrets is also referred to as Frigga's right-hand maiden. She is depicted as a virgin with free-flowing hair and a golden band around her head. She protects the chest that holds footwear belonging to the goddess Frigga and guards it with her life.

Fulla may be depicted as a servant, but in some forms of manuscripts, she holds a much-elevated position. She is mentioned in a poem as a sister figure to Frigga, and they describe the women as the sun and her sister.

While Norse mythology and Asatru beliefs seem to favor the strength of the gods, there is no doubt that the female goddesses play a major part. Asatru teaches us that life is a mission to find knowledge and truth and that even the mightiest Gods can learn from their female counterparts.

The Norse God family tree is an interesting one. It includes Ymir, the original ancestor of Giants, who fathered a series of Giants. They then became the ancestors that produced the Gods that are featured in the ancient history of the Asatru. Scattered among the descendants are different species, like the horse and cow, who also played their part in forming the religion we now recognize.

Chapter 4:

The Sacred Asatru Calendar and the Rites that Accompany the Dates

---

The sacred ceremonies that accompany the Asatru calendar are named Blots (pronounced bloats) and are named from the ancient term for the blessing. 8 major Blots are held at specific points in the year to celebrate the passing of the seasons. Asatru is an agriculture-based religion, and each Blot celebrates the transformation of the Earth that transcends the land and affects our souls.

The calendar below is representative of the Asatru blessings that are compiled from different Germanic sources. They are not meant to be precise or rigid, but should be celebrated with flair by individuals and groups alike. The following dates and practices are the most popular ones and are normally held at the closest weekend to the date given.

After all, Pagans embrace the work ethic and leave the weekend for partying!

Yule or Winter Solstice December 20th to January 1st

Christians have hijacked this celebration and made it their own, but traditional yuletide celebrations date back way before the emergence of Christianity. It is a time for feasting, giving gifts, and celebrating the point of the year when the wheel of the world is at its lowest point.

Food and drink are left to placate the restless dead who ride fiercely at this time of year, along with elves and other magical creatures. It is believed that they should be warded off or invited in to share the hospitality of the home. The 12 days of Yule are normally spent baking goods that double as decorations before they are consumed by the family and guests.

It is also traditional to burn a yule log overnight to represent the light that burns even in the deepest darkness and provides life to all who live there. The ashes should then be used as amulets or other forms of protection for the rest of the year.

Disting

Known as the charming of the plow, this ceremony takes place when the first moon of February occurs. Sweden is the only country the feast is considered regular.

Ostara March 21st

Also known as the Spring Equinox, this ceremony is a feast to waken the Earth. The Christian Easter traditions have absorbed the ancient rituals and claimed them as their own. The hare is a holy beast of Ostara and the original source of eggs that are painted and hidden from children. Fires are often lit on hilltops as revelers sing and dance while joining in the celebrations.

May Day or Walpurgis Night April 31st to May 1st

This Blot celebrates the Viking fertility celebrations and has been adapted to include the Swedish saint Valborg who lived in 710 AD and was a niece of St. Boniface. The heathen practice of burning bonfires and singing traditional songs herald the arrival of spring. Young males are encouraged to gather flowers and greenery from the woods and use them to declare their intentions to females they wish to connect with. They decorate the homes of their future partners and wait for them to respond.

Midsummer Around June 21st

Also known as the Summer Solstice, this is the second most important Bolt of the year, with Yule being the first. Midsummer is one of the most vibrant celebrations of the year, and worshippers will create model Viking ships and fill them with flammable offerings to the Gods and burn them as they set sail. In Viking times, the celebrations centered on the fact that the brave warriors had planted their crops to ensure their families would eat, and now was the time for adventure! They would sail off to foreign shores to do battle and bring back the spoils of their endeavors.

Midsummer is a time for riotous bonfires, eulogies, and celebrations involving phallic symbols like the Maypole, which are representative of the fertility aspect of the ceremony. This is a time for adventure and bravado when the heart beats faster, and the soul shines brightest.

Frey Fest August 1st

Also known as Lammas, this festival is the first sign that the time of harvesting is about to happen. Loaves of bread are baked in the female form to represent the Goddess Freya and are then shared and eaten. Wells and springs are also decorated to celebrate the life-giving qualities they give to the land while the warriors are abroad.

Frey fest is a Bolt to welcome back the weary warriors and remind the celebrants that the time for work is upon them. The next few weeks will be filled with harvesting and readying the community for winter.

Fall Feast September 21st

Also known as the Autumn Equinox, the Bolt centers on the second harvest of the year. There is a central bonfire that is fueled with the bones of dead animals that have been stored away for winter, and all the families in the village light their hearth with the central flame. After this, all other flames are extinguished, and the villagers share the bond of a shared hearth.

Livestock is often included in the celebrations, and there is a real feeling of community. In ancient times, if you were alone and unprepared for winter, chances are you would perish. This ceremony is about unity and shared experiences.

Harvest Fest October 31st

Also known as Winter Nights and All Souls Eve, this is the start of winter and a time for contemplation. All animals who are not expected to survive the coming cold weather are killed and preserved, and worshippers take the time to reflect on ancestral forefathers and the lives they led. It is also common practice to save the last bale of hay or sheaf of grass for Odin and his companions. This ceremony is performed by the female member of the family and signifies her elevation to the leader of the home.

Winter is the time to practice indoor work and recreate the traditional crafts that our ancestors mastered. The ancient people didn't regard death as a surprise or something to be mourned; they considered it a natural fact and celebrated this fact by remembering those who have gone before.

There are multiple other lesser feasts and days of remembrance throughout the year. Some Asatru followers will embrace them all, while others will take part in just a few. Remember, this is a religion of choice, and how you celebrate it is personal.

Chapter 5:

Norse Magic

The Norse people were famed for their magical practices and believed this was the way to connect to their gods and the spirits that accompanied them. They sought to connect their soul to the Gods and take control of their fate by living a life filled with honor and virtue.

Much of the information we have today is derived from works known as the Sagas and the Eddas. These were scholarly accounts of the practices of the heathen religions that were found in burial mounds and other sacred grounds around the continent of Europe. However, the accuracy of these accounts has been questioned by modern historians who have suggested that the Christian authors would be prone to bias and negative attitudes towards the Asatru faith.

What we can learn from these accounts is that magic was an everyday part of life for ancient Norse peoples. Their animistic view of their faith meant they acknowledged their Gods and Goddesses, but they also believed that all objects, places, and creatures had a spiritual essence. As such, they understood that working with the power of nature would help them guide their destinies and improve their soul with the knowledge gained from their surroundings.

Ancient Norse society believed that magic was primarily "women's work," and men rarely carried out these practices. Even though Odin was known for his shamanic powers, the ancient Nordic men preferred to leave the Blots, rites, and rituals to women. These female practitioners were known as priestesses and often had the power to see into the future. Often, they would be accompanied by sorceresses, who had the power to speak and send messages to the spirits and invoke their involvement.

Male roles were more practical. The men who were left behind when their Viking compatriots sailed away generally dabbled in politics, agricultural matters, and the overseeing of any newly acquired lands and treasure. Those that did delve into magic were known as priests who, like their female counterparts, could communicate with the spirits.

Types of Nordic Magic

Seior

This practice is a combination of skills, and the women who performed them were often revered and feared in equal parts. They were named the Volvur and would often live alone as they were powerful oracles who needed solitude to practice their craft. Occasionally they would band together with other Volvurs and their assistants to travel to villages and practice their arts. They would perform rituals to communicate with the spirits and lead the villagers in rousing chants to raise their energy.

The Volvur would often reach states of altered consciousness and openly speak to the spirits. This enabled the villagers to pose any questions or communicate with the spirits of their ancestors who had passed over to the spirit world or Hel.

Spae-craft

This type of magic was more practical and involved healing abilities as well as psychic communications.

The term spae means to prophesy and foretell; it is believed that spae-craft was a more positive form of magic and involved healing the body as well as the soul!

Galdr

Historical evidence notes that galdr is one of the more vocal forms of magic used by ancient Norse practitioners. They can be used for many purposes like cursing, invocation, and energy inducing. The tone and rhythm are very much decided by individuals, while the text often comes from the stanzas quoted in the Eddas. The original words of Odin or any other preferred god can be combined with rune-based poems or personal chants to perform galdr. The intention will often shape the form of the galdr.

Runes

Way before the emergence of the Latin alphabet, runic alphabets were used to write communications between Germanic and Norse people. The god Odin himself believed in their mystical properties so much that he spent 9 days and nights impaled on a sacred tree to gain knowledge of their meaning. On a ninth night, the runes appeared to him at the base of the tree, and he was set free.

They consist of signs and symbols that represent various elements of the natural world and represent animals, destinations, and objects. Some runes are abstract, and their meaning can only be divined by a skilled practitioner of the art of casting runes. They are traditionally carved or painted onto stones, fragments of bone or wood, and should never be cast by novices. To cast a rune, you must have in-depth knowledge of their power and meaning.

Berserkergangr

This type of magic is the forerunner to the modern word berserk. It involves elite warriors and Vikings channeling a state of fury and using it to become the disciplined fighters that believed victory was theirs. Some historians have described the Viking warriors as uncontrolled, rage-filled barbarians who would kill without mercy and pillage for no reason. The truth is they were one of the first examples of elite fighters who were devoted and dedicated to their cause.

They used the state known as gangr or fury to fuel their psychological fighting skills by practicing berserkergangr. The warriors would pray to Odin to channel his energy through them and alter their physical state. This would release much-needed adrenaline and hormones to allow them to become the ultimate fighters in a battle.

Viking warriors would also invoke their spiritual animal spirits by wearing the skins as part of their battle dress. This is why images of Viking warriors are often depicted swathed in the furs of bears, wolves, and boars. Although it must be pointed out that Icelandic winters were very cold, and the furs would also have helped keep the men warm!

While these types of magic can be adapted to suit the users' needs, there are some more specific spells available to study. In the late 1900s, an Icelandic poet nicknamed "Skuggi" or the shadow in English, claimed to have access to pages from a magical book that dated back to early Viking times. He spent 30 years recreating the spells he claims were within these pages, and in 2015 the results were published in English for the first time. The Sorcerer's Screed can be purchased directly from the Icelandic Magic company or Amazon.

Chapter 6:

Sacred Tools Used to Practice Asatru

Humans stand alone in the world of mammals because they use tools to make tasks easier. They have a history of adapting and improving the tools they used to become more adept. The same statement can be applied to worship and performing rituals. While most followers of Asatru will tell you there is no real need to use tools to connect with the spirits and gods, it is human nature to enhance the experience by employing tools.

When practicing rituals and magic, it can be difficult to leave the realm of the mundane world and step into the sacred realm. Changing clothes and using certain tools and aids help us propel our minds into spiritual mode! They set the stage for your departure from the physical Earth and your entrance into the interface that connects you to the gods and their nine worlds.

Tools also help us form a bond with our ancestors as they represent the respect we hold as modern practitioners for ancient ways. Some practices of Asatru have been moderated to adapt to the times we live in; for instance, animals and other live sacrifices are replaced by gifts of wine and food.

Here is a basic list of tools that can be useful to novice practitioners:

Alu

While Alu is a rune that is used in a spiritual context, it can also be used to describe any alcoholic drink used in rituals. It is thought to be the derivation of the Anglo-Saxon word ale and is used in many rituals to celebrate the occasions being marked. Asatru followers believe that alcohol inspires creativity and poetic lyricism, which brings them closer to the gods.

Blot Bowl

Also known as the bolli, this ceremonial bowl is used to contain sacred liquid. In ancient times this would include the blood of a sacrifice which would be caught by the bolli before traveling to the 9 realms to appease the gods. These bowls can be as simple as a wooden bowl carved from oak or maple, or you can choose to use a more elaborate vessel. Etsy and Pinterest both have highly decorated examples for sale that include runes and ancient symbols associated with Asatru.

Drekki

This tool is a horn fashioned by hollowing cattle or sheep horn to form a drinking vessel for hot liquids. This tool is used in the ritual of sprinkling and to share libations within the group.

Gandr or Stave

This is a tool used to cast a gandr shot. This is a curse used by the bearer to indicate displeasure with the recipient. The gandr is also a wand or stick used to cast a spell of love over potential partners. They are made of beech or ash wood and carved with magical symbols and runes. Elemental staves can be used to perform rituals depending on the seasonal requirements and the time of the year. Homemade staves will be fashioned to reflect the needs of the user, while some practitioners may prefer commercial staves available from online resources.

Incense

There are different schools of thought regarding the use of incense in Ancient rituals. Some people believe the ancients used oils to hallow their environments, while others believe that tobacco played a part in the ceremonial blessings. Modern practitioners use essential oils to enhance their rituals and make it a personal experience.

Glass

In ancient times it was a major status symbol to have a glass bowl or cup. Including a glass, the receptacle can make your rituals become an elevated event and attract the attention of the gods.

Harrow

This is an alternative to a traditional altar. In most ceremonies, it can help to have a focal point to work on, and a wooden altar will suffice. However, those who want to follow the more original ways will prefer to build a harrow. This is a heap of stone used to represent the hearth of the home, both inside and outside of the house.

Iron Knife

Iron is often described as the holy metal, and having an implement made from iron will help ward off evil and ill-meaning spirits.

Milk

Using full fat or whole milk as an offering can attract the attention of the goddess Freya and her handmaidens. It can also be blessed to create a healing draught to cure human ailments.

Oath Rings

These rings are specially crafted from wood, bronze, pewter, or steel and feature Nordic themes like the bear, wolf, and dragon. They can be unbroken or worn as a bracelet that wraps around the arm. The ring should be dedicated to the gods and goddesses before being used to make an oath. We are aware of how important oaths and promises were too early Asatru believers, and any oath that is sworn on this ring is binding.

Spindle

A narrow-rounded rod used for hand spinning when used in rituals is representative of the goddess

Frigga. She used the spindle to represent women's strength and might.

Wreath

This is a living form of the oath ring and should be made from the materials available, depending on the season. Apples and evergreen branches should be used at Yule, Salix branches at Ostara, and sambucas at Midsummers.

Yew Tree Branches

Closely related to Yule time, this is the tree of death and, as such, can play a major part in rituals. It is important to note that the wood and berries of the tree are poisonous and should be treated with care. Never use yew in a house with infants or pets that can gain access to the tree. The wood or berries should never be burned as the smoke can prove fatal to those in the vicinity.

Never feel you need to have all these tools or ingredients to start regular practices of Asatru. Begin with a simple glass of water, which is the life-giving liquid we all need, and hail the gods! Lift your glass and address the spirits of the Norse ancestors that walk alongside us every day.

Asatru can be practiced daily, and the main point is to embrace the spirits and gods as part of your normal routine. Thank them for your experiences and ask for their council for the future. Help shape your life with these Nordic influences and embrace their ways!

Chapter 7:

The Significance of the Afterlife

Think about the concept of heaven and hell in Christian beliefs. Most religions will tell you that the possibility of being punished after you die is a reality you should consider as you live your life. They tell of fiery pits where your soul will be tormented as opposed to the radiant life of those who go to heaven and spend their afterlife sitting in the presence of God. While this may seem a simplistic way of looking at death, it has two main outcomes and gives Christians a glimpse at what may lie ahead.

Asatru has a more complex view of the afterlife. When the body dies, it is acknowledged that the soul or parts of the soul take different journeys. Pagans believe that there are four destinations for the soul that include Valhalla and Folvangr. These two destinations are part of the belief system upheld by Asatru followers, but they don't include Helheim and Helgafjell like some pagans.

While Norse traditions talk of the souls of warriors going to Valhalla with Odin or to Folvangr with Freya, they also talk about Hel as the destination for souls not lost in battle. Because of the similarity to the Christian concept of Hell, this is often depicted as a place of punishment. In reality, the Asatru religion doesn't pass judgment on people in life or in death.

Hel is simply a place to go when you die. It is not unpleasant, and it is ruled by Hela and is the ultimate final destination of the dead. While the Asatru is not judgmental, there are some crimes that would require punishment in the afterlife. Murderers and oath breakers are considered the lowest of the low, and a special place of punishment is available for their souls. This place is called Nastrond and is the final resting place for tortured souls where they can be tormented until Ragnarök, the final days of Earth.

What is Valhalla?

Anybody who has seen or read anything about Vikings and their beliefs will have heard of Valhalla and the ultimate end to a warrior's life. Valhalla is the hall of the fallen with a golden roof and made from spears and shields. Odin, the master of Valhalla, welcomes the souls and bodies of the dead of those he deems worthy of fighting alongside him. Its gates and entrance are guarded by ferocious wolves, and magnificent eagles soar above the hall looking down on its inhabitants.

Within the hall, the Viking warriors spend each day fighting battles and perfecting their art alongside each other until they retire for the evening nursing their wounds. As the evening comes, they find their scars and wounds are healed, and they are restored to full health, ready for the following day's battles.

Now it is the time for feasting and drinking! They are attended to by the 12 handmaidens of Odin known as the Valkyries. They are noble, beautiful maidens who spend their evenings bringing food and drink to the warriors that live in Valhalla.

The food they served was supplied by the boar Saehrimnir who is butchered every day and then restored back to health, much like the mighty warriors he feeds. The wine they drink is supplied by an equally magical creature known as Heidrun, a goat whose udders produce a tasty mead rather than the more traditional milk. The Valkyries tend to these animals and ensure the warriors have an endless supply of food and drink to fuel their enormous appetites.

Unfortunately, the souls of the warriors are not called to Valhalla for fun! Odin has amassed the best and most successful fighters for a reason. He is preparing for the final battle, Ragnarök, where he and his mighty warriors will face the ultimate opponent Fenrir the Wolf, when they will ultimately perish.

What About Reincarnation?

Asatru beliefs do vary from culture to culture, and you can choose your own beliefs about how you will spend your personal afterlife. Reincarnation can be affected by using family names, and Asatru believes the possibility of being reborn will be within your own family. When you name a child after a relative that has passed on, you increase the chances of them inheriting the soul of the person they are named after. For instance, if you name your son after your grandfather, it is believed he will be reincarnated into your son's body.

It is frowned upon to name children after relatives that are still living as it is deemed as casting a death wish for the person involved. Some souls are said to go to a place named Disir, where they will live in funeral pyres and watch over the families that have left behind.

What Happens to Believers Who Choose to Devote Their Life to Other Gods?

If you have chosen to give your life to Freya or Thor, then Asatru believers can be called to spend the afterlife with their favorite God. Most of the deities have heavenly halls, and you can be summoned to help them with their daily routines and become part of their household. Most of these halls are found in the 9 worlds that make up the heavens that form Norse mythology.

As we begin to understand more about Asatru and its beliefs, it is becoming clearer that how we believe and choose to live is our choice. If you want to spend your afterlife looking over your family and being there for them, then you will. If you want to spend it chilling with Thor in his heavenly halls, then devote your life to him, and chances are you will be called. The Asatru doesn't dictate where you spend your afterlife, so as long as you avoid Nastrond, you should be okay!

Chapter 8:

The Values of Asatru

P agan religions have often been accused of defending anti-values and failing to provide a set of values for their followers to live by. Society seems to thrive on chaos and immorality while dismissing the simple tenets of right and wrong.

Asatru values are based on three basic concepts. They are governed by the intellect of Odin, the sound judgment of Thor, and the honorable beliefs of Tyr. Asatru teaches us that the correct place for moral judgment is positioned between the heart and the head. It also promotes the idea that as human beings, we are fully equipped with common sense to distinguish right from wrong and make our own decisions.

The Eddas chronicle the lives of the gods and show us examples from their lives that illustrate the set of values they believe in and how they have influenced their actions.

The modern followers of Asatru have adopted 9 simple values that are taken from the Odinic Rite with the hope that members of the faith will adopt some if not all of them. This is not meant to be a moral code or a guide on how to live life. Instead, they should be regarded as a recommendation based on the good name of the faith.

Nine Noble Values of Asatru

1) Courage

It would be difficult to find people who don't recognize the need for courage when dealing with daily life. We are all faced with moral dilemmas that call for us to follow blindly, even when we know we don't always agree with the outcome. Living honorably can be difficult in modern society, and it takes real courage to stand up for honor and truth.

2) Truth

Two aspects of the word truth are applied to Asatru beliefs. There is the personal code of being brutally honest with yourself and others and shunning actions that you wouldn't be able to own up to. Respecting your personal honor and living a truthful life is an important part of upholding Asatru beliefs.

The second kind of Truth is the one with a capital T. This truth is based more on religious and moral principles. Asatru recognizes that we each have our truths, but that the search for the ultimate Truth should be a lifelong quest if we stop searching when we stop believing.

3) **Honor**

While it is listed at number three, honor is the basis for the whole of the Asatru value system. It is, however, one of the most ephemeral in its meaning. Put simply, honor is a combination of all the other values and then some! If you can live your life with honor, you will have no cause for regret.

4) **Fidelity**

This is a value often defined by its association with marriage. Marital fidelity means being true to the vows made to your partner, but can often be misconstrued as only applying to sexual fidelity. However, when applied to Asatru beliefs, it is important to understand the sacred bond members form when they join the faith.

The rite of entering the faith is similar to marriage vows, and the relationship between members and the gods is just as important. That is why fidelity to ancient ways is essential.

5) **Discipline**

This value is better described as self-discipline and is required to develop a sense of personal honor. As already discussed, modern society encourages the rejection of moral codes and promotes a lack of self-discipline. This type of discipline is intricately linked to fidelity and the strength to avoid outside influences.

6) **Hospitality**

Ancient travelers were accustomed to hospitality and would expect to be welcomed into some form of shelter wherever he went. This was the basic fabric of society and formed the basis of communities.

In the modern world, there is a different way of practicing hospitality. Some heathen religions believe it is acceptable to disrespect other faiths and beliefs and treat their members with disdain. Asatru believers are expected to treat other people with respect and dignity.

Recognizing that having a different belief system is a personal choice helps Asatru communities work hand in hand with other faiths. When we pool our resources, we become a functioning community that works together successfully.

7) Industriousness

The gods are not fans of laziness! Both vocational and non-religious lives should be filled with hard work, done with care, and a sense of pride. Asatru believers get involved and give their whole selves to a project. Consider the origins of the faith. Vikings weren't known for sitting around contemplating their navels; they were known for being vital and living each day to the full. Get involved and be industrious.

8) Self-Reliance

The ability to stand on your own two feet and make your way in the world may seem to challenge the value of hospitality. Surely if we all managed to look after ourselves, then this other value would become redundant? In truth, hospitality wouldn't work if everybody refused to exercise self-reliance and relied on others to provide aid.

Being self-reliant is all about taking charge of your own destiny. Don't rely on society to provide you with a roof over your head or a weekly income. Make sure you take responsibility for your own morality and honor. There are too many people riding the gravy train that society supplies; don't be a passenger; be a driver instead.

9) **Perseverance**

Having the strength to pick yourself up and start again when you fail or encounter a problem is essential. The only way to achieve greatness is to press on until you succeed. Asatru believers understand that internal strife is just one way individuals can fail; they also know that hard-fought battles are the best way to achieve personal honor. This requires courage, self-discipline, and strength. The Asatru community has faced hardships and recognizes that the only way to create a stronger community is to persevere.

These simple values may seem obvious, but Asatru believes that as a unit, they encapsulate the wisdom and perspicuity of the Ancient gods.

Chapter 9:

Asatru Rituals and How to Perform Them

Rituals are very personal experiences, and Asatru beliefs encourage their followers to make them relevant to their own needs. The most common ritual is called a Blot, pronounced "bloat," and can be performed at any time for a variety of reasons. Ancient rituals involved sacrifices and blood, which is where the term Blot originated. Some people still use the term despite its bloody connotations, while others have renamed the ritual Faining.

The origins of this ritual epitomize why modern society sometimes fear Pagan rituals. They hear the word sacrifice and immediately conjure up images of dead animals and bowls of blood. Back in ancient times, most people were farmers of some kind, and it made sense to offer gifts of animals to the gods, while today's society is vastly different. Modern rituals offer gifts of alcohol like wine, mead, and ale.

Consider the differences between the two societies and the rituals will make more sense. Ancient Norse people would slaughter an animal and use it to feed their family and any guests that were visiting their home. When they slaughtered an animal, it was to invite the Gods to feast with them in the same way as they would invite guests.

Modern society concentrates less on the food aspect and instead offers the Gods an alcoholic beverage. Modern Blots are designed to share enjoyable experiences with the gods and welcome them into our world.

How to Perform a Blot

Blots are multifunctional and can be adapted to suit your requirements. The ritual described below is known as an All Gods Blot and will give you a basic example to help you connect to your Gods whenever you need inspiration.

Tools You Will Need

- An altar: This can be as simple as your kitchen table or a wooden bench in your garden. You may prefer to build a stone harrow as your sacred point. Using natural materials will help you feel a connection to the Earth as you strive to connect to the heavens.

- A Hammer or a symbol that represents a hammer
- Blot bowl
- Horn
- Knife
- A branch of wood relevant to the season
- Your offering, maybe wine or mead

Now is the time to invite people to join you for your ritual. Ask them to keep an open mind if they are non-believers and embrace the experience. Make sure you have a healthy mix of serious Asatru believers and newcomers to keep the ritual fresh.

Hallowing

Now perform a cleansing ritual using water and the branch of seasonal wood you have chosen. Hold your arms aloft and invite the Gods to join you.

The Procedure

The main celebrant, often known as the priest or priestess, should hold the horn aloft and offer the Gods a libation. Hold the hammer over the horn or make the sign of the hammer (an inverted T) in the air above the horn before blessing the four points of the compass. Use an incantation to invoke the God Thor to the Blot and ask for his help to banish all evil and unwanted entities.

Use this type of chant: "Mighty son of Odin, we use your name to invoke your presence and ask that you witness our joyful celebration of your powers and might. We dedicate this special day to your honor and invite you to partake in our bounty. Hail to the Gods and may their presence be felt among us.

Reading

If required, a reading from the ancient texts can be used. Try poetry or song and invite the other celebrants to join in your incantations.

Call the other Gods

This is the part of the ritual designed to attract the attention of the other Holy Powers you want to join you. Everybody should face north and call upon the spirits and powers you want to invoke.

The Rede

You should now be aware of the presence of the Gods and their spirits. The Rede is a purpose of declaration and the time to ask for what you want. Maybe you need help at home because someone is sick, maybe a call for knowledge as you prepare for a tricky time at work; the choice is yours.

The Giving

Now is the time to pour the offering into the bowl and horn and place it on the harrow. Once it has been blessed, take the items and pour the wine on the ground. Offer it to the Gods with thanks and ask them for the protection of Thor's strength and the gift of Odin's' wisdom.

The Closing

Now is the time for celebrations! Declare the Blot is finished and proceed to drink the remaining wine or mead with your fellow worshippers.

The Sumbel

While the Blot is the main ritual, the Sumbel is also an enduring ritual used by the Asatru community. A typical Sumbel, there is an introduction followed by a round of drinking dedicated to the gods and goddesses. There is a further round of drinking dedicated to ancient warriors of Norse times and ancestors gone by, followed by a rousing round of drinking, singing, and poetry.

Profession

This is one of the most important parts of the Asatru religion and is often performed when new people join the community. It is a personal commitment to Asatru and should only be performed when the person involved is fully invested in Asatru beliefs. The oath taken to join the religion is based on a promise to follow the ways and beliefs of the gods and lead a life that is true, honorable, and brave. There are traditional texts that can be used, or the person making the profession can craft their own.

The ceremony should be performed by a leading member of the community and should involve the oath ring. This ritual can be compared to a marriage or maybe a confirmation ritual in the Christian community. The vows that are made are binding and sacred and should not be broken. The ceremony should only be performed with prayer and reverence.

The Bottom Line

These are just three of the more popular rituals and can be performed whenever you like. If you are interested in more elaborate rituals that accompany the traditional blessing ceremonies, there is plenty of information available. Every blessing has associated rituals, and every one of them should be performed with joy and love.

Chapter 10:

Living as a Pagan in Modern Society

Modern religions can be a positive force in some people's lives, and if that is the case, then great, embrace the beliefs you have and embrace them. However, not everybody is happy about the form that some religions have taken. Society places huge pressure on people and their families with the belief that religious followers are the only people who have 'moral' children and strong family units.

The problem with most religions is their insistence that all your downtime is spent at worship. Sundays should be a day of rest, yet we are told that attending church is the only way to praise God. Shouldn't we be spending time with our families on Sundays and celebrating our family ties? Surely an hour spent playing games with your kids is worth more than a dozen sermons from the pulpit.

The media is filled with stories of religious intolerance with people experiencing ostracism or being shunned by their churches based on their sexual beliefs and personal preferences. Religious teachings often contain values that clash with modern teachings and can seem to frown on the advancement of science and medicine.

If you feel frustration at traditional teachings and beliefs, you may find the Pagan way of life gives you more freedom of choice. But does it fit in with your busy life in modern times? Well, the simple answer is yes! More than other religions, Asatru and other pagan religions allow the follower to make their own choices about how they worship. They don't preach; they don't insist on you are following strict rules, and they give you the tools and information to live an honorable life.

Modern paganism can give people a new way to live. Rituals and embracing the nature that surrounds us can make our spiritual sides blossom, but is it practical?

Here are ways to embrace modern Paganism into our everyday lives:

The following suggestions aren't all-encompassing and should be used or set aside depending on your needs.

1) Understand the Phases of the Moon: There are four primary Moon phases known as the New Moon, First Quarter, Full Moon, and Last Quarter. Consider how the different phases affect your mood and how you feel.

2) Respect Your Surroundings: We are just guests on Earth and should treat it as a sacred place. Recycle your rubbish and grow food whenever possible, and cut back on your environmental footprint.

3) Lead an Empowered Life: Stop being a sheep! If you believe in something that isn't popular, dare to say your piece. Stand up for your beliefs even when it involves going against the grain and be your own person. Society is always encouraging us to be individuals, but then social media and other outlets seem to repress any original ideas.

4) Make Every Day a Thankful One: When was the last time you gave thanks for your life? Not specific events or gifts, just life in general. Try taking a minute to take stock and give thanks every morning. The Pagan life is filled with Sabbats and special days to give thanks, but you can make every day special. A simple morning "thank you" to the Gods will fill you with a sense of wonder and respect for the gifts we are blessed with.

5) Be Honorable: When you make a promise, keep it. Simple, right? Consider how many times you have helped somebody in the last month. How many times have you gone out of your way to help a friend, a stranger, or a member of your family? Sometimes we can get too tied up in our own lives to recognize when someone needs us. Share your bounties with others and live a more generous life.

6) Turn the Mundane into Magic: Just how much magic do you have in your life at the moment? Most people will answer "not much," but paganism helps you change that. Cooking an evening meal for yourself and your family may seem like a boring everyday chore and about as far away from magic as you can get. Try cooking from scratch and using fresh ingredients for your meal.

Hold the fresh produce in your hand and consider how it got to your kitchen. What are the processes involved that produced the meat that will feed your family? Grow your own vegetables, and you will understand exactly how much effort it takes to produce a tasty carrot!

Creating a dish for your family should be magical and sharing the experience should be an incredible occasion. Make sure you are all involved in the process by having an interactive meal that doesn't involve electronic devices. Share your news and have real conversations while you enjoy the meal. Food should be shared and respected as it fuels the body and the soul.

7) Consider the Impact You Have on Others: While paganism encourages you to be your own person and believe in what you say, it also encourages people to be respectful. Harsh words and insults are not part of a pagan doctrine, and followers are encouraged to be kind to others. Be encouraging and supportive to other people, and you will experience feelings of contentment and satisfaction.

8) Rediscover Hospitality: Modern society has enabled us to become reclusive and communicate from our homes. We have more virtual conversations and friends than real ones. The art of conversation is in danger of becoming extinct as we text, message, and inbox our friends. Arrange for people to get together at your home whenever possible and bake for them! Share the love and respect you have for each other. Sometimes the greatest gift you can give is your time.

Most of all, you need to recognize your shortcomings and continue to grow and learn. As humans, we will never know it all; there will always be something more to learn. Don't just rely on your normal sources of information; seek new and unexpected experiences that you can learn from. Life should never grind to a halt, and we should never stop growing.

Conclusion

Now you know there is nothing scary or evil about paganism and its associated religions. In fact, there is more love, respect, and honor in Asatru than in normal practices. If you feel this mad, bad, and sometimes sad world we live would benefit from more joyful experiences, then you may feel Asatru is for you.

Good luck with your journey, and don't forget to call on the ancient gods for company!

Sources

http:www.icelandmag.com

http://www.odinsvolk.com

http:www.asatrunews.com

http:www.ravenkind.com

http://www.aminoapps.com

http://www.theasatrucommunity.com

http://www.norsegodasatru.com

http://www.realmofhistory.com

http://learnreligions.com